Finally "At Last"

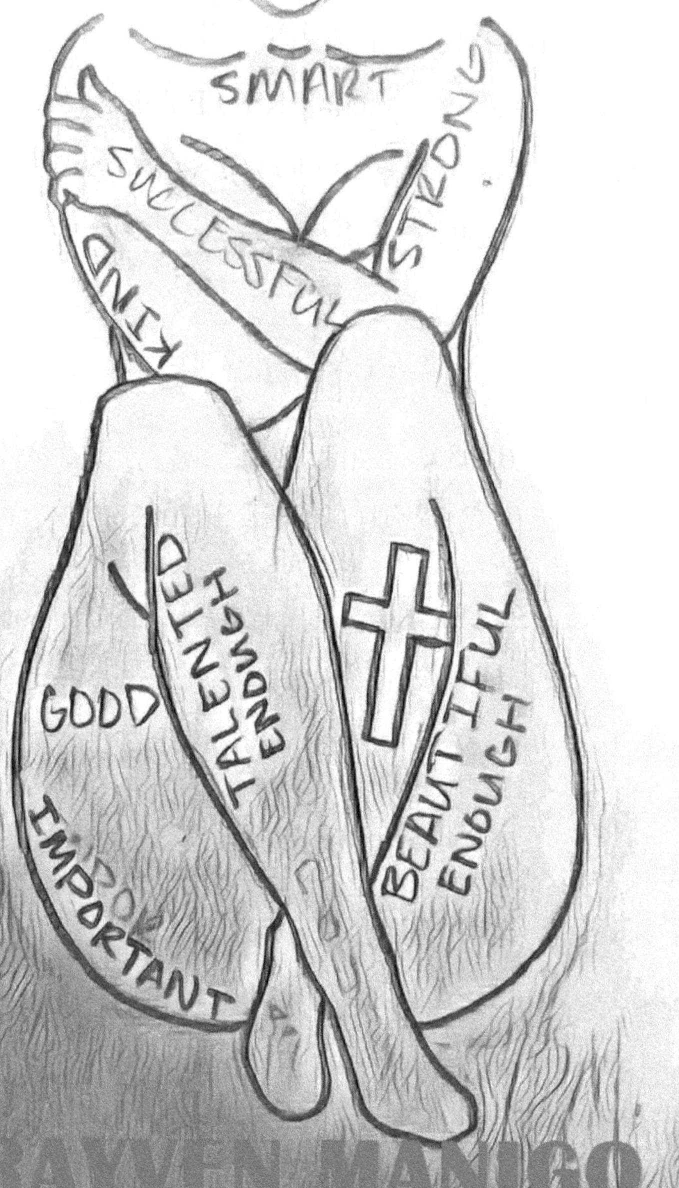

RAYVEN MANIGO

FINALLY "At Last"

By Rayven Manigo

Cover Illustration by Braylen Mosley

Cover Created/Designed by Jazzy Kitty Publications

Logo Designs by Andre M. Saunders/Jess Zimmerman

Editor: Anelda Attaway

Co-editor: Rayven Manigo

ISBN 978-1-7349014-5-0

Library of Congress Control Number: 2020913436

ACKNOWLEDGMENTS

Philippians 4:13 NIV: I can do all this through him who gives me strength.

What an amazing journey this has been. This seemed surreal, not knowing if my friends and family were just telling me "wow, this is great" to spare my feelings, or if it was in fact really great. Only time will tell!!! There were times giving up, saying I'm done, making excuse after excuse took total damnation over my life. But how many people know God will send someone to encourage you? He will send someone to help you see YOU GOT THIS!! Your faith may be tested, but your testimony will be great!!

I am thankful for my village, my daughter is absolutely amazing, she constantly asks, "Mom are you writing something for me?" Of course darling, her charisma, growth, development, sweet demeanor and sensitive yet bubbly personality makes me go through each day wanting to be the best!! I am an amazing mother, nobody has to tell me, she does constantly!!! This is for you my love!!! When God is in it there's no limit!! My parents, WOW!!! The best people in the world, the most giving, caring, and unchanging!! God made my parents special for me because nobody else would spoil me the way they do.

At 34, years of age, I still, we still, and forever will spend time together. From phone calls, to trips, and everything in between. I am forever and eternally grateful for the parents God blessed me with. It isn't taken lightly, nor is it taken for granted. They are two of my biggest cheerleaders, remarkable people!! God, I thank you!!! To my brother, you are the best brother and uncle on this side of Heaven!! We can always depend on you for anything, babysitting LOL!!! Thank you for being my "Bubba."

To all my supportive friends, thank you!! I wouldn't be who I am today without your listening ears, your advice, and the genuine love you show consistently, doesn't go unnoticed!!!

Last but not least, to my man, my sugar foot, my entrepreneur! I love you more than words can say!! Writing was a hobby, something to do when I couldn't go to sleep, when friends were going through, when trouble transpired in my life. However, it is much different now, the vision displayed and the foundation set. It becomes a purpose when it knocks you off your feet and wakes you up at night. You constantly tell me, "Baby, you can do it!! Stop doubting, you got it Man!!!" Ahhh!!! Only he can give me those pep talks to encourage my soul. Which brings me here!!! FINALLY!!!!

Best Regards

DEDICATIONS

To the daughter God saw fit for me to welcome in my life. This is for you, go after whatever you dream, you're the only one that can hold you back from accomplishments. Be confident, Be tenacious, but most importantly Baby be you.

Love you, Mommy

TABLE OF CONTENTS

TABLE OF CONTENTS

TABLE OF CONTENTS

INTRODUCTION

FINALLY, AT LAST. . . Occurring at the end!! The title speaks for itself, removing doubt, embracing change, and going with it!! Whatever happens, happens!! Whatever will be, will be!! But we miss every chance that we don't take. We miss the mark every time when we don't attempt!! Finally, here I am ready to take the chance and embrace writing!!

Writing began many years ago, the understanding that writing takes my mind off of many different avenues of the world. Writing allows me the opportunity to express myself with words, instead of actions. I am thankful for the gift!!

Often told, "You have what it takes."

But there's something about honestly believing, Girl, yes you do!!!

A LETTER TO MY GIRL

Dear Baby
Life is all about, Commitment, Chances,
Highs and Lows
Resentments come, Sacrifices to Endure
As sure as the Wind Blows

Disappointments, Grief, Setbacks, Milestones,
Obstacles even

But life is about Learning to Dance in the Rain,
And seeking Positive
During a Difficult Season

Life continues to Change
Even for those that are Strong
But what I Strive for you is
To Count Your Blessings
And learn to Admit when you are Wrong

Be Better than I,

Be Stronger than I

When adversities Arise,

Count your Joy, Mount up, you'll see Why

Treasure each Day

As if it were your Last

Endure the road ahead it helps

Overcome the Past

Know that whether Right or Wrong,

I love you MORE each day

I pray that God helps you

Find your Own Way

Through God, seek Courage

And with me, Support

I want you to Listen Closely,

As I teach you How to Sort

Keep your Prayer Life Strong
That's where Peace is given

Back away from Negativity,
Learn the difference Between
Forgetting and Forgiving

Place the Good HIGH ABOVE the Rest
But remember,
The Bad will help you withstand
The NEXT Test

All throughout your Life
I want to Show you Love
by His Grace

I want to be as Supportive as I can
While you can still
Touch my Face

I want to be a Solid Foundation
In which you Trust
Develop a strong Backbone,
That parts a Must

God continues to prove me
Worthy of you
He allows EVERY DAY to be
Better with you

My steps are further along
Through Him,
I have the Courage to Carry On

You are the Best Thing
That ever happened to me
And NO MATTER what comes my way
You see the Best in Me

You make me Smile
When inside at times I Hurt
You make me Thankful to be on
God's Amazing Earth

You are my Reason
And that's Enough for me
Thank you so much Baby Girl
FOR MAKING ME A MOMMY!!!

MY LOVE

You are so Inquisitive,
Seeking answers from your Million Questions
We have countless Heart to Heart talks
Stemming from Life Lessons

At times,
Your questions can be answered with a
One Word Response

At other times,
It takes me a few moments
To create a few words
Without Nonchalance

A question you asked Before
I left it Open for Many Reasons
Because at times the answer Changed
As my body sought the Different Seasons

Well, here I am
Ready to take part in your question
Ready to give you an Honest Answer
Allowing my feelings to Show Expression

You asked me. .
Why daddy and mommy aren't together
Here's the TRUTH,
Daddy allowed Mommy to fall victim
To Lies

He only thought of himself
Followed behind alibis

I've always Guarded your Heart,
Never ALLOWING it to Break
Because I know how that feels behind
Countless Mistakes

Daddy chose a Different Path
And Honey that's Honest
He didn't VALUE FAMILY,
And he often BROKE his Promise

Well, let me Start Over, at the Beginning
DADDY LOVES YOU and I LOVE YOU TOO,
But at the beginning there wasn't ENOUGH LOVE
Between us two

We were young. . .
Without care of what could happen
We didn't take Precautionary Measures,
Intercourse WITHOUT the Wrapping

Sometimes you Follow your Heart
And other times your Head
Sometimes you allow actions to show,
NOT what was Said

Your Daddy and I will Remain
The Best of Friends
We will be AMAZING co-parents
And give you LOVE until the Bitter End

As I close
Asking for your Forgiveness
Asking that you will Forgive
My lack of Common Sense

You DESERVE a family
And I didn't give you the Chance
But One Thing I will say is
No matter the Circumstance

Mommy LOVES her Baby Girl
All the way to Heaven and back, times two
And there's NOTHING in the Whole World
That I WOULDN'T DO FOR YOU

This isn't to Bash your Daddy
Or make you Love him Less
It's an opportunity to go into my Secret Closet
With TRUTHS I Must Confess

Troubles come and our Paths Cross
Different than we Hope
But we remain Faithful
And learn how to Cope

I didn't give you the Family you Seek
And for that, I carry the Pain in my Heart
I pray that you Understand
And allow God to create a Chapter
Starring you and me Sweetheart

PERSEVERE

Being a Single Mother
Wasn't in the Cards for me
I had a nice Foundation
Designed by my family

My parents been Rocking for years
Before my Maternal and Paternal grandparents Utilized
Love in the most Amazing form

So again,
Why did this happen to me?
Why did I pursue something
Without the "I do"

You see?
I rushed without realizing the Consequence
I decided to use my "cookie"
Instead of Common Sense

I guess the Future didn't include
White Picket Fences, a White Gown
And something Blue

But Sleepless Nights, the Breast or the Bottle,
Y'all I HONESTLY didn't have a Clue

As a Single Mother you find Strength like
Never Foreseen
You Break your Back almost to make sure
Your kid/kids have Everything

At times, playing dual roles
Mom and Dad
Making sure your kids never fall victim of feeling
Inadequate and Sad

The desires of family is still Embedded inside
But this Independent Mentality and that Pride

You've done it So Long
So why change now?
Because everyone deserves those things listed before

Everyone deserves the Fairytale Ending
And what God has in Store

Sometimes it's about getting out of your Own Way
And Realizing everyone makes Mistakes
Each and Every Day

People will always Ridicule
But as long as you ask God
To Forgive, Repent and Live by His Rules

You too may be a Single Mother,
But not for long
Trust and Believe the right man
Will come along

Let's not even mention the Pain
The Inadequacy will take a Different Form
And the Pain a New Name

See what happens next
Will take life to a Whole New Dimension
Trust and Believe it's all about God
And His Intentions

As a Single Mother I may have Strayed Away
From the Course
I may live my life Filled with
A lot of Pain and Remorse

But one thing that I hold True to my Heart
Is my Beautiful Creation,
That's been a BLESSING from the Start!!!

I'M CONNECTED

Connection:

Being linked, a relationship in which a partnership is developed and a journey begins

Let me Transition within my Journey
So that I may Honor you
The Journey to Peace, Love, Perseverance, starts here
It's a place of Refuge, Sovereignty, Grace
And New Mercies appear

A place of Love, Gratitude, Support just to name a few
In you I find my Reason, my Purpose
And my Strength becomes New

God the words Flow so effortlessly
Because I'm speaking of You
The clouds don't Cover up the Sky,
There are still Peaks of Blue

Wednesday's and Sunday's
Are my most Favorite of the week
Because, I gather Touching and Agreeing
With two or more Shouting Hallelujah!
And souls are Reached

Oh God!!
I never knew a Love like this before
Honestly, the feelings can't be adequately explained
They encompass so much more

You Forgive me,
Even when I have yet to Forgive

You make my days ahead Greater,
Not because I'm Deserving
But because of Your Will
The plan over my life is so much bigger
Then I could've created

God that's AMAZING,
I'm so glad You are my Creator
The journey, even though there's been Bumps
Along the Road

The Ending is better than the Beginning
Because You never left me;
Even helped Lighten the Load

God,
Words seem Insufficient when describing You
There's more than Enough Feelings,
But the Adjectives just won't do

I've made Countless Mistakes
But You DIDN'T Count Me Out
You prepared me for my Next Transition,
Giving me a Reason to Shout

I'm Growing Stronger in You,
I can tell more now than before
Because being at Abundant Love Fellowship Church, The
vision is Clearer that ever more

You've aligned so much
And I'm GRATEFUL Beyond Measure
I'm Touching and Agreeing with Your people,
The journey now begins with this Hidden Treasure

GOD'S WORK

Take it from a man who spends most of his time Looking
at the back of ones' Crown
The clippers begin to "buzz"
And the decision about the Fade…
Or inch of the Blade goes Down

A barber is defined as someone who. . .
Cuts, Shaves, and Trims as their occupation
But this barber, God gave Vision
And it's become a Beautiful Revelation

It's amazing how my Hands are Insured
And my Clippers are a Blessing
There are times that I'm reminded of His Grace;
Listening to clients Confessing

When you sit in my Chair,
The atmosphere is unlike another

Partnerships are made,
Brotherhood built' like one to the other
As a barber I've learned my Hours
Don't Start NOR Finish like everyone else

At times, the shop sees more of me
Than I actually see of myself
People are Connected from
The First customer to the Last

The experience isn't Interchangeable,
Meaningless or Countless remnants of the Past

This lifestyle chosen
Different than many Other Choices
Gives me a range of Clientele,
Ones with Baritone or even kids with
Tiny, Squeaky Voices

All from different Walks of Life,
Circumstances and Situations
But after the Final Spin,
They glance and thank me for
My Wonderful Creations

Ahhh!!!
Being a barber is a Gift from Above,
I'm dedicated to the Craft,
Every cut Designed with Love

WHAT IS LOVE?

Love is when outsiders view your connection and attraction after years apart as "beautiful"

Love is when you gaze into someone's eyes and forget the whole world is going on around you but you don't care because your focus can't be distracted!!

Love is accepting someone at their worst because the best is going to outshine everything that you have been through

Love is when you don't want to hurt them so you do everything in your power to make sure that doesn't happen

Love is when you realize being without them is the hardest thing you would ever do and you aren't willing to experience that

Love is chasing dreams together and building foundations stronger than ever

Love is knowing in life good happens and bad happens but weathering the storm together is all your heart knows

ACCEPTANCE

What are you willing to accept in a world full of the unknown?

Are you holding on to something that doesn't accompany value?

Should you disconnect yourself because of the mistrust and unwavering guilt?
Bury your thoughts in the darkest of times and the ever so uncanny what ifs

The real question is the acceptance has to be from within
Nobody can tell a person how to love or even how to make amends

The guilty pleasure of the less than desirable attributes
Is that something that you can see following suit?

I imagine the acceptance speech follows the gift
You shouldn't accept something without getting your desires right?

Or should you accept the halfway, almost potential, and hope the other half comes forth eventually?

I don't know I'm still traveling alone without a man
Or am I just tired of accepting the halfway, potentials, and I'm seeking more than

I guess I would love to have someone capable of being great
Someone I can build with, someone who can relate

Someone that loves God and his communication stimulates my mind
Someone who devotes words but his actions are right on time

Someone who desires to build a strong foundation, built on trust
Showcasing his love for me and my love for him is a definite must

All these closet romances are not how God intended it to be
I'm just trying to be a virtuous woman who's as precious as a ruby

Yea, that's what I'm willing to accept
What about you?

YOU

At your Lowest Point
You find Strength like no other
You find Growth in your Heart
That Overcomes the mere Complexities of another

You find deep roots Embedded in places
You never thought to Seek
You find the Truest form of Life
That's not made for the Weak

You find the will to Carry On
Where Dark Clouds used to Shadow with the Pain
You find reasons when you didn't sense the desires
Before to Dance in the Rain

You find you are girls that's a Hell of a Beginning
You find the Truest of things
And that Showcases Mending

You used to be in a Deep Place
That only God could bring you out
Now you are withstanding Tests and Trials
And distancing for the mount

As you get ready to take off your Dreams
Following along
Never forget where you are Now
And where the Past went Wrong

DETERMINED

Have you ever been so determined for Greatness,
Envious of less?
The Process kept you reaching until
You reached your Best

The best you,
The more determined as such
The one person even the Naysayers and Haters
Couldn't touch

Determination, Perseverance, require some Skill
Success comes to those that Continue
When others can't Feel

The feeling of actually reaching that Desirable Thing
When at first you wanted to give in,
Listening to the Negative that others often Bring

You see,

Determination requires someone Tenacious,

So to speak

Someone who doesn't Stop

Because the road gets Rough

But it Relates to those whose Course

Gets a little Tough

If we didn't Focus on the Future

Because the Past wasn't Bright

Then we wouldn't see all the Great Things

God has hidden from your Sight

When you are Determined

Your actions Show when words Can't Express

Determination Striving for more than your Best

I hope you are Determined!!!

RAW EMOTIONS

Raw Emotions unbeknownst to anyone's Fairytales
Of what should be
Just your Emotions lying face down on the Surface
And your Bitter Thoughts with Purpose

Are you too Sensitive?
Well, maybe it's not that Bad
You are entitled to Every Feeling which ranges from
Happiness to Sad

When your Heart is Broken
There's only Raw Emotions to shadow through
Don't lose those, let them come too

When you Hold Back there's so many Feelings
That may deem too Aggressive
You don't want to Misconstrue your Raw Emotions
And have them MISS the Message

The truth is,
Men and Women differ some Attributes not alike
Women can be naturally Sensitive, Emotional,
And at times the Jealous Type

Men can be increasingly Territorial, Insensitive,
And Judgmental with the increasing Hype
The reality is, even though men and women differ
They do agree on Some

When you find the Right Person,
Your Heart begins to connect as One
When the main Focus is God
As the man follows His direction

The woman will follow the man's Leadership
Without discretion
There's a Message brought forth in every Relationship
Some find their Love after a Strong Partnership

Others find Love by Law of Attraction

Their Eyes met with instant Satisfaction

Give Love a Chance even after Heartbreak

You may end up sharing Raw Emotions

Even after the Mistake

COVERED

I've heard it a Time or Two
Be patient Love, let him find you
I always Envisioned what he would be
Something different, Unexpectedly

The mere Glance of him
Will make me Feel Secure
The warm Embrace from him
Erases all Doubt and Fear

Those words that I've heard before
Prepared me for what God had in store

Ummm…the Unexpected,
The never Chartered Experience
More than a mere Coincidence
But more of his Existence or is it Persistence?

When you don't feel Butterflies
Because that feeling usually Subsides
You feel Security
That only comes with Purity

Let me explain. . .
You meet someone and your Tummy begins
To feel Disconnected
You know this man is Sent from somewhere,
But a little Expected

That's the man you thought you wanted
But those Butterflies go away
And his personality Taunted

See what happens is
We go after the Excitement
But in reality there has to be More
Something more Inviting

The man that brings Security,
Covers you like a Blanket
This man doesn't bring Butterflies,
Something your tummy can't get

He brings about Protection, Stability, a Foundation
He brings something so Meaningful
It eludes most Conversation

He brings a Difference
That at times can't be Explained
He is devoted to God,
And not afraid to Proclaim

The feeling doesn't last for a week or two
Honey, this feeling is so deep it Lingers inside of you
So listen, when they say be Patient let him find you
Or you won't get to feel that Security
He wants to Provide you

EMPTY

Empty; containing Nothing,
Vain, Bare, Vacant
Unfulfilled by Circumstance a bit Desolate

When the feeling of Emptiness
Is Encompassed with Fear
The Emptiness Pours into your Soul
Moving from first to forth Gear

Uninhabited, Unoccupied, Hollow Inside
Being unequipped with Thoughts/Fears
Insubstantial Pride

What happens when the mere thought
Has an impact so severe?
Isolating begins to direct your life
Without a Steer

Well, I have some Good News
In spite of the Situation
Cast all of your Anxiety on Him
Because He cares for you

No matter the Emptiness you may feel
He wants to uplift you
At times we put so much Power in man
That God can't perform because we limit His stance

The Deliverance comes from getting
Out of our own way
Allowing Him to Heal our Broken Heart
Bind up our Wounds every day

Emptiness is a State of Mind
Not a Final Destination
It's temporary, allow Him to guide you to your Blessing
From Empty to Fulfilled!!!!!!

FEAR

Fear an often Strong or Unpleasant Emotion
Causing one to avoid something or someone
Fearing the unknown, taking steps around,
Avoiding unchartered Territory

Being against, or Accompanied with Doubt
Fear will have you in a place so Unsure,
So confused without

Without the Motivation
Or the Ambition to go forward or pursue
At times, we question the Fear as a Value

Let's begin here. . .
Fear is often Strong or Unpleasant
At times, we get so accustomed to Complacency
No one wants to chance it

When we charter something Unfamiliar,
Unforeseen, it is Scary
We avoid it like Licking all around the Sundae,
Yet, leaving the Cherry

We miss the Mark because
We get Comfortable with our Thoughts
We dismiss the problem
As if we are a Thief, avoiding being caught

See, fear will have you staying in the corner
When there's Room to Grow
It will have your Heart saying YES,
But your mind yelling NO!

Once fear Consumes
And questions begin to Ponder
The only thing left to do is
Chance the Wonder

Honestly, Fear puts things in Perspective
If you take a Step Back and Look
If you didn't want to Experience it,
Why even Analyze the Book?

BEATING HEART

Words, can't describe the Feelings
I have for you
The way my Heart Flutters
When I'm Missing you

When my Feelings Grew,
I didn't think they would Last
Thoughts about how we got to this Point,
Moments in the Past

Our Embraces were always Followed
With Harsh Goodbyes
We NEVER Worried about Deciphering
Truths from Lies

Our Relationship then is much different
Than now
Now comes with Strong Feelings
And I'm unsure how

How we were before things didn't matter
When I didn't care who called
Because my heart too Strong to Shatter

Too tough to Break Down the Walls
To even care enough
Too afraid to know if
I would ever be Good Enough

As a woman that Caught your Attention
A woman Different from the Rest
Unsure if I should Mention

The lady in the Story
Who Endured to the End
Because she knew what was to Come
Was much Better than what Had Been

Truth be Told
My FOREVER was a Bit Shady

I didn't know I would soon enough
Carry your baby
That's where the story gets a Little Deeper
We went from Lovers, to Parents, to Friends…
Keeper?

Out of order was definitely not the way
I Envisioned
But if we did things by the Book
Our Love may not be Mentioned

I will break that down a Little More
The day I became a mother
I never knew what God had in Store

He turned my Playful ways
And Fulfilled them with a Gentle Touch
With Longing for more than the Illusion
I dreamt so much

Family you say means more to you too
Family is unlike anything
Someone else could do

Family is an Understanding
That NOTHING is Perfect
It's taking the Good and Bad
Knowing in the End it's Worth it

It's realizing you don't want
Another person to take your Place
Because it doesn't Feel as Good
Getting what's left of the Embrace

My views Changed and my Love different for you
Now I see
Life isn't always a Pretty Fairytale
But it could be!!

LESSONS

Have you ever just been Tired?
Tired of Lame People
And Tired of their Countless Lies

Oh!! Pardon me
This poem may be more of the Truth
Than I've shared before
The Expressions will be a Little Different
Since there's more to Explore

Hmm… Let me start by saying
I'm normally not this Petty
I'm usually the one who is Hurt
The pain doesn't show; Emotions Unsteady

Well, today my friends
The Petty reveals the Underlying Truths,
You without a Shield

The anger is like this,
A man that only thought about the
Physical Stimulation of your Body NOT your Mind
The one that depended on you
For the Smallest of Situations,
Acts like you are the one Unkind

Have you ever held someone down
And been everything they needed?
But in all honesty, your Soul is Crying
And your Heart Internally Bleeding

I'm Perplexed with being that person
That gets Played in the End
Promises Broken and Continuous let downs;
A heart that Struggles to Mend

People often Proclaim Trust your Heart
And Follow it,
It will Lead you to your Desire

But my Heart shattered into
Several Pieces
And my Soul feels like it's on Fire

The harsh reality is
This putting too much Emphasis on
Their every word makes you Vulnerable
But doesn't that also make life Worth Living
And things more Tolerable

Well, I held on to the thought of
"Who knows what the future holds"
Well, evidently it didn't hold much as my Trust
Is Growing Cold

Some people just Use and Take
As much as they can
The Undeniable Truth is
You were more than he could Stand

Men can only Show you
What they've been Through
They only want what's a Challenge for them,
Yes, that's true

What I didn't realize until Recently
It seems
Maybe I was Too Available
And he became Bored with those things

Maybe my hair didn't Touch my Back
Unless it had the help of Brazilian
Maybe my eyes didn't Sparkle
Unless he wasn't near them

Maybe the bedroom was Lacking
Something more Exotic
Hey!! Who am I kidding
Those things don't keep a man loving someone
That's been there all along

If he wants to Leave
And Pursue other options,
Where's the wrong?

Well, he shouldn't Make Love to you
Sunday and Monday to start the week
Then Declare he is with someone else on Wednesday
So to speak

Well, being Vulnerable has its Moments
But being Tolerable has its Value
If you tolerate the Mistreatment
He wants to put you through,
Then there's no point of him Valuing you

NOW OR NEVER

We utter the words Now or Never,
As crazy as it seems
Can we really be done?
Or will the Love Wither Away
Just like Water Moving Upstream?

I guess, I'm amazed this time being Different
Than the Rest
What makes it so Unique,
I ask through this Quest?

Does the now ever come?
I'm still waiting to see
Or does the never talk Hold
And the Rest is History

I've dreamt a reality where you are by my Side
But I also Envisioned the thought of being
Someone else's Bride

Well, this is how it goes in a Fairytale Story
She gets her Prince Charming
And they Live Happily ever after
Gloating in their Glory

But this is a very different Beginning
The chapters are Overlapping
And the beginning is in place of the Ending

At times things happen Out of Order
Leading from One Mistake moving to Another
But the great Promise that God has for you and me

He rewrites out Story,
Removes Hurt and Replaces it with Victory

You once told me. . .
There's no negative Thoughts in your Mind
But as the days go by I'm Forced to Believe,
Some thoughts are of a different kind

When I want someone
Or something to the Point of Craving
Nothing can stand in my way
There's no point of the Saving

We go through life with the idea of,
it'll always be there
But there's no guarantee,
no day is promised, so let's move on from here

Will it be Nor or Never
One must Decide
Let the Ego go
And put the Pride to the Side

UNTITLED

The mere thought of your Touch,
Creates a Picture in my Mind
It takes me to a place that I Love to Travel
From time to time

Let me share my Desires with you
So you can see what Intimacy
Without the Physical can do

I desire to be Touched
But further out than a Reach
I desire to be Fulfilled in ways that
Help Mold, Motivate, and Teach

The desires I dream about are Quite Different
You see
My Desires don't just begin here
They are Much Too Deep

Let's paint a series of Understanding
To assess
Beginning with an Overseeing of Everything
Nothing less

Picture yourself Smiling
When nobody else is in the room
But those thoughts Feeling your Mind
And your Body Consumes

When I say nobody else makes me feel this way
It's true
Nobody stimulates my Body, Soul, and Mind
Like you do

I was in Denial at first
There's no way I can feel Dampness there
I mean Shit the boy hasn't Touched me,
He isn't even here

But Oh No!!
That was so far from the Real
The mere thought alone has me saying,
"I can't deal"

I mean will it always be this way?
That's the part I'm unsure of
But I will say

My thoughts of Intimacy aren't always Physical
Often times it takes me to a place
More Typical

Daydreaming, taking me to a Faraway Land
With the Brazilian blowing in the wind
And Toes in the Sand

See, the thought of you
Makes me Travel through Dimensions
It makes me feel Unapproachable, Untouchable,
By others, did I mention

It Shuts Me Off from
The Outside World
It's Crazy because
I'm not even your girl

It creates a Path so clear,
I see Far Ahead
But I am not sure if the Feelings are Mutual
So instead. . .

I fall back and allow you to
Make up your Mind
But just know the most Precious thing we have
Is TIME

S&S

There's this guy who came into my life
After a difficult Season
Right after Heartbreak,
My life uneven

The Trials that came before
Made Love seem Unfeasible
The person that I became unlike any other;
Inconceivable

He said all the right things,
"Give me a chance and I can show you I am real."
Well, I've heard that Phrase too many times
And my Heart wasn't ready to Feel

See, I questioned his Purpose
Before knowing his Last Name
I portrayed Judgment to Avoid him
Bringing More Pain

I gave the Cold Shoulder,
You know, One Phrase Responses
When he wanted his Name to weigh heavy
On my conscious

To speed things up a bit
I decided to Embrace Change,
Totally Commit
What did I have to Lose
When I wasted time on the Wrong One?

Maybe giving him a Chance
I will recognize a Good One
Let’s just say, I’m glad I took that Leap
Because he provides Happiness
And Giddiness that I now Reap

Letting the past go
And slowly moving in the right direction
He gives me the best attention
And let’s not mention the affection

He Touches me without the Physical
He Embraces my Heart even in the Spiritual
This man a little younger than I
Brought Rainbows to my once Cloudy Sky

To be Honest. . .
I didn't think much of it at the Beginning
But my Questioning has turned
Into a Happy Ending

I can't Imagine where I would be
If I didn't take the Chance
To really Embrace Happiness
And Pure Romance

FINDING YOUR WAY

Countless days spent Wondering
Will I EVER be Enough
Will he see what's Right in Front of him
Or overlook it more than Once

See, I've put people on Hold
And Sabotaged others
Because I wanted my Family more
Then I wanted a Meaningless Lover

I've questioned my Worth
A few times Too Many
Simply trying to understand
Will this time be as Good as any

The idea of family is like this
Love is Shared, Romance Conquered,
And Eternal Bliss

God is Overshadowing everything
Between you two
Love is like an Ocean Flowing,
No need for the Canoe

The Waves at times come
And that's just Trying Times
Oh Yes,, there will be those,
One Must Realize

But back to what my Heart
Is trying to Understand
Why am I still Waiting on this man?

Well, let me Share some things about my Life
As a kid I have thousands of Memories
Shared with Mom and Dad
Never realizing what made the other children
Envious and some Sad

In certain Homes a parent is Missing
And a times a Step One is added
To support the Mission

Well, I didn't have this growing up
So I wasn't aware
That a stepparent comes in to Fill the Void
While the other isn't there

Well, I think that's where
My Vision gets Lost
Because I didn't see that in the Cards
At Any Cost

I saw the White Picket Fence
And the kids chasing one another
I saw my Husband on the Grill
As we shared Stories one after the other

I saw Trees, Flowers, and the Sun Shining
On the Lemonade

But what I DIDN'T see
Was the Thick Cloud beginning to Hover
Which leads to the Shade

Well, the story hasn't quite finished
And I'm not sure when it will be
I'm just making a Simple Promise to me

Whatever comes your way
Be Prepared
Because you can't go through Life
Living in Fear and Despair

Consider yourself done
When the time is Far Spent
And only then will you know
What they Truly Meant
In stating "find your own way"

PEOPLE SHOULD KNOW

Predicaments surpass Detriments of the unknown
You wonder when the Bow Breaks,
Will the Reaping become Sewn

For some, the Understanding is a bit Perplexed
If you wish
It's like an Illustration of consuming the Main Course
But secretly loving the Side Dish

Picture only feeling Good Enough
For this not that
But never more because that's not where
His Heart is at

Hmm… Let me see
If I can Paint the Picture Clear
Not caring what comes with the Honesty
Eluding the Fear

You Touch him in Places
Nobody else can Reach
Your Dedication to his Happiness is something
Only you can Teach

He misses. . .
Your Laugh, your Presence, your Walk
When you aren't Near

But he's become so interested in
Keeping up with Appearances,
A world so far from here

This Game can only be Played
With WILLING Participants
But somehow the Rules Change
Every chance they get

Let me attempt to Explain the Rules if I can
Making sure everyone gets the same Opportunity,
A chance to Understand

Behind closed doors, the Hugs tend to Linger
And the Kisses are so Sweet
Let's not forget the Softness of the Bed
And the White Fitted Sheet

The uttering of his voice remarks the following words,
"Me and her aren't together"
But it's amazing how his words are clear
Depicting Rainbows even,
But his Actions broadcast unusual Weather

The calmness of his Voice
Makes things seem More Real
But the mere Complexities and Levels of the Story
I can't seem to Feel

He whispers, "I love you"
In your ear So Clear
But he lays next to her
And draws her Near

See the reason the Side Dish tastes better
Than the Main Course
Is because the Heart is Left Broken
And now there's Regret and Remorse

On the Outside Looking In,
It may seem I'm Struggling to let him be
I've done that Countless of times
This ain't NOTHING new to me

But this time,
There seems to be a Slap in the Face
She's confessing her Love,
But he's still Missing your Embrace

Umm, some may Wonder
How you know this to be True
Simple, there's a thing called Text Messages
Shared between us two

He went after the Glitter
Hoping it shined Real Bright
But he only lasted so long
Before looking for the return Flight

The Grass was Greener on the other Side,
Yea, he felt this to be True

But when it is considered AstroTurf,
The surface is Nice
But the Roots Are of a Different View

People should know the Truth
About what he Admires
Nothing has Changed, one has to Accept
The way in which they Inquire

BE THAT GIRL

Girl, she's so much Prettier than his Ex
I overheard this Conversation
Between two girls from afar
In a Deep Conversation about a chic
That wasn't "Up to Par"

Be careful Baby because this one is
About to get Deep
I want to be able to Dive into this thang
Without caring about how Steep

See,
The chics talking were Mediocre at best
Portraying hand me down clothes
And no True Finesse

See,
It's easy to look at a person's Outer Appearance
And start to question
What went wrong during that Life Lesson?

Let's back up a bit so we don't get Off Course
We are so quick to Judge and Point Fingers
With No Remorse

Even though she may be Prettier than his Ex
Does she Weather the Storm… Next
Does she treat the kids like her own?

Does she pray for him,
Not having to adjust from Casting the first Stone?

Does she value his Goals, Dreams, and Desires?
Or does she hide behind friendly Smiles
And other Countless Admirers?

See the Struggle is simple at Best
She may be Prettier than his Ex

But she doesn't Measure up
When you place her Qualities in Position
She doesn't even have the "will do" condition

Geez!!! Beauty Fades,
Just like Rainbows in the Sky
Don't look back on Life and Question others
Why?

Don't be like the mediocre Gossiping Girls
With no True Intentions on Conquering the world

Be your own beautiful Inside and Out
Be the best you without Doubt
Treasure being the girl with the many Qualities
Because nobody can take that away;
No Capabilities

TAKE IT ALL IN

Self-Esteem, the reason some Struggle consistently
With the Misunderstandings from the Self-Reflection
I too, see the Mirror… Standing clear
And avoiding because of my Complexion

Am I too dark?
My skin has Marks and some Unevenness
But can I hide behind Mac, Sephora, Covergirl
Because of my Blemishes?

Wait!!! Girl, you go without Makeup
Throughout your Entire Day?
Woah!! That's a Struggle for me baby,
I wear Makeup in every way

You know it makes me feel like a new woman,
Boosts me a bit
When I highlight that brow,
I say Yessss Girl, that's it!!!

But has this merely started, my granny used Tussy
And wore deep plum Lipstick
But I, a Dove Girl step out
In bold Colors, Matte, extra Shimmer,

Yes, I am that chic
Some say are you Hiding
Because your Canvas isn't Perfect?

Well, at times I do
Because my attitude doesn't match me
Being worth it

The hype is. . ..
Some men Love being with women
Who look the Part

And if the Presentation were in some way Flawed
Their Feelings and Misjudgment
Would elude the Start

The decrease of Self-Love doesn't begin
At this moment

Did it start with the skinny models, their perfect skin,
Maybe because of their Own Flaws,
They didn't own it

To be Bare
Letting the world see the Real you
Is at times, Hard

People are so judgmental. . .
At times, Evil in that Regard
Even when you want to be Transparent
Jokes are often Heard

She's the girl with the big lips, nappy hair, blemishes,
They spread that word
Nobody seems to care about the Inside of your Heart
Or Soul, anymore

And we wonder why
There's so much Hate, Judgment,
When there's more to Explore

The reality is, we are all different Flaws;
Yes, you too
But we must never forget where the Heart lies
Within each one of you

From every Strand of Hair,
Every Wrinkle just right
To every Dimple that's in Plain View,
And the ones Out of Sight

Say a few Reminders in the Mirror
When you see your Reflection
Remember you are the Best you,
No Ridicule, No added Subjection

FRIEND WALL

Friend; having a Strong Like for
Or putting your Trust within
Some often say one they Call on,
Or even Confide and Depend

But see, there's a little something different
About the Friendships that I have
These ladies remarkable, ambitious, gifted
And all that

Let me share a little about my Friend Wall
We've been rocking so long. . .
Ribbons, Knockers, Ponytails, Nano Babies, Pagers
And All

When the streetlight was the Curfew we had to Beat
Long before the Eyebrow was Highlighted
And soon after the Acceptance of history
We soon Repeat

Ahhh!!! See friendships now
Are much different than before
We didn't have Social Media drama,
We just went to their front door

You see,
This wall is Built using about nine members
All of us are Different;
But wait we ain't looking for Extra Contenders

From matching Gaucho pants to K-swiss,
And even "Melissa's" we rocked all colors
Where every sport we are Winning,
That's right, beating Connally and many others

Distance couldn't make our Friendship
Nor Bond Break
From our Group Chats to our Birthday Turn Ups
Or even Casual Lunch Dates

Oh Yea, the late night drives to Corsicana,
Shhh!! Our parents still don't know
The consuming breakfast Taquitos from Whataburger,
Need I say more?

Ummm. . .
"Do you want your pizza crust?" a voice stated,
While we are all sitting at the Lunch Table

To buying dozens of eggs
And piling up in my mom's car,
You are right. . .
We will save that part for later

We grew Closer as the years Progressed
And our paths Intertwined

Now,
Our kids are playing together as we once did,
Walking a Similar Line

Our careers are even Closely Associated
As we are Connected to Students, Families,
Leaving a lasting Legacy

We will leave out the rest of the crazy stories
Embedded in my Memory

Yea. . .This Wall is Strong
Every person adds their own Flare
Like the Foundation of a Building,
You may not see it but you know it's there

I wasn't Blessed with biological sisters
So their Faithfulness is Real
Like when I decided to step out on Faith
Writing poetry they soon will Feel

Surprise Friend Wall this is for you
As I'm so Appreciative of your Support
And all the things that you do

There's so many places

You could be right this minute

But here you are Supporting my Dreams,

Oh, Yea, that book y'all are in it. . .

CHURCH LADIES

Did you see Sis. Maggie,
When she sashayed down that middle aisle?
Trying to get all the deacon's Attention,
Acting like she's been here in a while

Girl!!!! Her Dress is so Short,
I don't even want to assume

But the way she moved them Hips,
Someone should let her know
The devil ain't in this Room

Wow!!! Girl, she left the church,
Why did she even come back?

She should be on the corner of
Faulkner and Hood
Because that's where her kind is at

Jesus fix it!! Every Soul needs to be Saved
Yes, Chile that includes Sis. Maggie,
Here she comes let's Wave

Hey, Sis. Maggie how have you been my sister?
You know we've been Admiring your Outfit,
And those Edges Laid just right,
You know we couldn't have missed ya..

Oh. Hey Sisters
Everyone looks so nice
Well, it was because of Jesus on that ol' Rugged Cross
You know He already paid the Price

Somewhere between Genesis
And Revelations you can find this here. . .

You better learn to Confront others sin
With Truth, Love, and Respect
Before God draws you Near

Let's Back up and set the Scene
A little less Aggressive if we can
Because there's some little church ladies
In every congregation, understand

This Era is quite different than before
The Slip, has been Replaced
And the Dress no longer hits the Floor

But does that make her Praise different
And her Walk with God NOT Strong

Because instead of carrying a Bible,
Her Bible is displayed
Using an App on her Phone

She doesn't have those cute little Cover ups
To go in her Lap
And in her Purse you won't find Mints,
But you will find Mac

Her husband isn't attached on her Hip,
Actually her Ring Finger is Vacant
But that doesn't make her less of a Christian
She may be Single, she's not trying to Fake it

Ahhh!!! As a Christian,
I pose this very question
Did you have Bumps along the Road,
And learn from some Life Lessons?

The reason some people don't come
Inside the church
Because there is so much Judgment,
You guessed it. . .
Some are #churchhurt

The little gossiping ladies could Impact someone
And bring them to Christ
But their unwillingness to Intercede with Love
And cast away Strife

Could be the very reason Sis. Maggie stayed away
We should be very Cognizant of our Actions
And what we have to Say

As a millennial when we search within
You with arms open wide
It's because our Vision is at times misconstrued
Please don't hurt our Pride

Show us the way
And give us Real Life Situations
We know you haven't always been
The president of the Mission; Revelation

Yes,
It's okay to take us Down the Journey
Of your Life
Include how you ended up being
A Loving and Devoted wife

But don't leave out the Pain and Suffering

You may have endured

Because the Pain helps us Heal

From our own complexities, Reassured

SEE THE VISION, TRUST THE PROCESS

Vision: the state of being able to see,
Manifestation, Observation
Vision is discussed Abundantly
From Genesis to Revelation

Process: a series of Actions,
Steps taken in order to Achieve a particular end
From paying "rent" to 500 seats at a new Sanctuary;
ALFC I highly Recommend

When the devil has plans,
Remember God's plans are far greater
And exceed the Rest

Plans so Outlandish,
Start your Praise now,
The Vision within your Purpose
Stems from His best

Pastor
You consistently align the member partners
With the Word of Truth
Brought forth to God's people,
From those more Seasoned to our Youth

The Vision so Clear some may be Unsure
Or not too Familiar
In order to Position with the Vision
The Holy Spirit MUST Enter

Your Heart, your Mind, your Body, and Soul
As the Preached Word consumes you,
The Strength, Love, Trust, begins to Unfold

Jeremiah 29:11 resonates this. . .
"For I know the plans I have for you."
I have a few more
We will Embrace those too

Numbers 12:6

"I the Lord reveal myself to them in visions,

I speak to them in dreams"

But one must position within His divine Word

And it seems

Some use Vision Boards

For their own Visual Mind

Some use other Forms of Measure,

As they may be a little Pressed with time

When the Vision is brought forth

It always Connects with God's Mission

As two or three are Gathered Touching and Agreeing,

God encompassed within the Decision

From the ushers and nurses, ministers, deacons,

creative arts, youth to the choir alike

We MUST EVEN Love our Enemies,

YES, even those you Feel DIDN'T do you Right

The Outreach of Love through our ministry
Shares Hope and Promise
From every Blood Washed Believer,
To those seeking Guidance; Honest

It helps those who are Lost
Or being Cast Away
God help us Minister to their Spirit
While helping them Find their Way

God is Increasing and Elevating us
One by One
And even Collectively

We are Growing as a Church
Both Inward and Outwardly

Don't quit Pushing until you see things
Start Crumbling
Strength made Perfect

God is Trying to Infuse you,

Hook you up, Elevation necessary,

Because you are Worth it

Proverbs 29:18,

"Where there is no prophetic vision the people cast off restraint, but blessed is he who keeps the law. . ."

GOD MAKES NO MISTAKES!!!!!!

NAPPILY EVER AFTER "MOVIE"

Natural

Ancestors

Products

Permission

Youthful

Webster defines Nappy as "of hair, informal, sometimes offensive, kinky, naturally coarse, and tightly coiled just to recount a few. . .

But does your "Nappiness" define the more natural you
When you hear, "Can I touch your hair?"

Umm. . .
Do you want to know if it is Real, a wig; spare?

People get so accustomed in melanin women
With Brazilian, Indian, Peruvian. . .
From 18-26 inches
Please don't cut my Wefts

Yes, keep it this Long. . .
Straight, Curly, Wavy,
The list goes On and On and On

Embracing the Natural
Really promotes Growth; Confidence
Use positive Affirmations if you Wish,
Sticky notes Compliment

The Texture and Curl pattern,
WOW!! Perfect Combination
Twist out,
Bantu knots,
Flat twists,
Pin up; Creation

When you change it up,
Stares begin to Surface Curious
Because your hair was just. . .
Hmm; Mysterious

Don't let it define who you are,
Personality
It's all about the Inner you,
Self-actuality

People will Voice their Opinions
Whether it's Long or Short, Fried or Dyed
To your ears or down your back with Malaysian's
Help; Guide

The most Comfort you Feel
May start with a Haircut
Ahhh!!!!! the Breathable sense,
Unmatched, Indescribable; Strut

Wear the biggest Earrings
And tightest Girdle you can find
Dress up in your Fiercest outfit,
Please leave the Bonding Glue, Thread, Tape; behind

The air will feel different
and your attitude will match
The natural you begins now,
unsnap, unfasten, and release the latch

Dare someone to stare, gawk, and question
or even release their opinion
Because baby you are killing it,
naturalness; dominion

Natural glow, Pigmented, Sassy, Classy,
Sexy; Wild
Your **ancestors** would Love you this way
Honey-Chile

You do not need **Permission**
To Feel Free; Unrestricted
Buy as many **Products** as you need
A world without; Limit

So. . .

Be **Youthful**, Declare, Decree; Forever

No limits, no Boundaries,

Happily Ever After; Clever!!!

***This poem is based on the movie "Nappily Ever After"!!!**

MY MISSION

Innocence; Lack of Knowledge, Purity, Blameless;
Child Forced, Utterance
If you tell I will hurt you,
Voice a different Pitch; Reconciled

One may relate in a multitude of ways; Familiar
From the Unknown,
To knowing your Perpetrator; Silent Killer

Encompassed in Fear, Mistrust,
Followed by "why me?"
Disgusted, Confused, Sorrowful, Empathy,
Many partnerships, Transient sexually; Promiscuous

Avoiding, Doubt, low Self-esteem, Inconspicuous
Rebellious, Risky, Isolated; Impossible
Most talented, Scholarships, Bachelors, Masters, PhD;
Unstoppable

The past doesn't determine the Future,

Advance

The hurt won't Stop the Strong;

Stance

The Best is yet to come;

Progress

Realize that before doesn't Align with now;

Process

Determination, Focus, God;

Vision

Overcomer, Conqueror, Strength;

My Mission

TRANQUILITY

Tranquility; Calmness, Peace, Serenity
Understanding God's promise,
Fulfillment, Purposeful; Divinity

Jude 1:2:
Mercy, Peace, and Love be yours in Abundance
For God gives all these things Pressed Down,
Shaken together, the drive encompassed

Quietness, Harmony. . .
You dare to Dream
Breathing it in,
Seclusion as it may seem

From Adversity, Trouble, Danger, Desolate
To Protected, Secure, Focused, Determined, Concentrate
From Worry, Confusion, Drama, Chaos; Bothered
To Joy, Comfort, Blessed, Our Father

First Peter 5:7:

Cast all of your Anxiety on Him

Because He Cares for you

Be Encouraged my sister,

God has a Mighty Plan for you too!!

FAITH

Faith; Strong Belief, Confidence, Support, Connection

Hebrews 11:1:

"For Faith is the Assurance of things Hoped for. . ."

Conviction His Protection

Faith is Evidence that God is there

The mere thought of His anointing;

The ever Present Help; Omnipresent, everywhere

We often times Lose Sight because of hindrances;

Tested

By those Adversities, Stumbling Blocks, Obstacles;

Soul Never Rested

Complacent, Comfortable, Afraid,

Unchartered Territory

But how do we get to the Testimony without the Test;
Story

Faith is Knowing, Believing, without Seeing;
Invisible
Miracle worker, way Maker, Healer,
Provider, Mustard Seed;
Biblical

Faith is Understanding that even in the midnight hour,
Mind Restless
It's already Worked Out,
MY GOD; INVESTED!!!

STRENGTH

Strength; in Particular, Skill,
Strong Suit Advantage
A few Examples with you in Mind,
You are built for this; Never Mismanage

Independence, Drive, Charisma, Dedication to Amaze
Through Setbacks, Drawbacks, Turbulence; Uneasy Days
Remember a few things that I've had to Analyze
Take every day as a day to Prosper; Realize

The Strong even have days
Where NOTHING seems Right
Where things just don't Fit
And NOBODY Understands; Hindsight

Where Frustration sets in and Negativity comes along To add more Insult
When things are So Crazy your Vision Unfocused
As a Result

You question things
You've never thought to Question before
You Replay the Should, Could, Would. . .
Like a song on Repeat once more

Strength isn't Trusting that Life will be Perfect
It's Learning to be okay
With the Small Misfortunes
Because your Dream is Worth it

Being strong isn't only the Physical
As some Try to Explain
So adjust from the Obstacles, Minor Setbacks
And Elevate; Proclaim
YOUR STRENGTH!!!

REKINDLE

Rekindle, Realign, Excite, and Revive,
To bring back the Lost
Why should one Revisit, accept again. . .
Do so at What Cost?

Your paths crossed before, Accidental
Or even for a Divine Reason
Just like Flowers Grow and Wilt,
During a difficult Season

There's some Promise in the Word Rekindle
You see
Don't take for Granted Feelings, Time, Partnership;
Decree

Your Love for one as you've
Exhibited before
Because there's no time like the Present
To fix mistakes; Restore

When you Walk into someone's Life
Do so without Regret
Because in all Honesty their past may be the Reason
Y'all met

Why do you Rekindle with someone
You easily Let go?
Was the Breakup Anticipated or Expected,
Does the other partner know?

Was baggage Involved,
Moving from one to the other?

Did one partner Forget to Mention
Trust Issues, Past Hurt,
Before things went further?

I would say only Rekindle when one can be Sure
That the future Looks Brighter
And through Love and Commitment
Both Feel Secure. . .

FORGIVENESS

The process of Forgiveness doesn't happen Fast
The Rehearsal of their Actions,
Replaying in your Mind. . .
The Hurt, Image, the Past

God Heals you First,
Ushers you into the State of Forgiveness
But the Process at times Grueling
And there's no sense of Swiftness

The pain doesn't just Transition to Happiness
As you Desire
It turns from Pain to Frustration,
Anger, Grief, Misunderstanding. . .
Ignites a Fire

Forgiving begins internally,
God within your spirit aligns
And in order to forgive
you have to allow the feelings to heal with time

God has a way to turn the Misfortune

To where you Love and Forgive again. . .

There’s NO Time Limit

But there’s Healing to Obtain

CONSISTENCY

Consistency; Regularity, Stability, Fairness,
Constant Unchanging
Words reflective of an action,
Encompassed from Engaging

When a person is Consistent it builds Character,
And Promise
Inconsistencies are what keeps us Complacent,
Let's be Honest

If I'm a Consistent person,
Someone Reliable and such
I will be the person Looked up to,
Agreed with, Uplifted, but how much?

Hmm. . .
Let's break down Consistency for a Moment
Being Transparent you DON'T Gloat,
You Strut, you Own It

Knowing without a Doubt things WILL Work Out
Because of your Desire
Remembering where there's Smoke
There's bound to be a Fire

Being Consistent in Daily Living
And even Relationships
Be ready, your Devotion will take you
From Partnering to Leaderships

Do not Conform because of the Heaviness
Of others Instability
But continue to Transform
Because of your Own Capability
BE CONSISTENTLY YOU!!!

DISCONNECTED

Disconnected, Detached, Disengaged, Isolated
All words meaning to be
Apart From or Without;
Confiscated

But is the Disconnect brought forth
Because of Differences
Or is it something that can be Worked Out
Through Communication and Experiences

At times we Disconnect because our Circles
Become too much to Handle
And our Paths are Avoiding, Words Misconstrued
And Situations at times Mishandled

Ahhh. . .
Take a step back and uphold the Disconnect
Because it helps us find our Own Way, Opportunities
And Chances, Embrace without Regret

You see, being Disconnected is like
A Conversation on the Phone
It was Real Good at first,
But then there's that Dial Tone

I'm sorry the person you are trying to reach is
Unavailable. . .
She's too busy Reflecting, making sure the Disconnect;
Purposefully Attainable

Remember when you are Disconnected
From something or someone
Connect with the Reason it had to be Done

NEW CHAPTER

I've gone through Life settling for Mediocrity
Never reaching Full Potential
Because of Impatience and the Reality

I never knew what it Felt like
To go the Distance
Getting scared, Close to the Finish Line,
And in an Instant

The Course was Changed
And the Race left Unfinished
Because my Thought Process
Didn't INCLUDE me Winning

But this time around I decided
To take a Chance quite different
I didn't even read the Warning Label
Because the RED FLAGS weren't needed

I stepped out of my Comfort Zone
To try a New Beginning
But here I am Contemplating the Worth
Based on the Ending

When he said,
"I don't want to Fight for you and that's Sad."
I again felt like Steering away
Because the thought alone would make anyone Mad

But you see,
In learning that, everything ain't my Fault
And some people Run Away from the Truth
Because being Hurt is what they Thought

You can't Teach someone How to be Loved
You can only Show
Especially when they take Past Hurts
To Current Relationships because that's all they know

Pointing the Blame at a person
Only shows Inadequacy
Something that person is Lacking Inwardly

From Rejections, to What If's,
And other countless Remnants
From Chastisement, to Love Fading
Because of Resentment

Normally people Fight for those
They would Love to Keep
And if your Soul is at Peace
And your Heart NO LONGER Weeps

The Chapter ends here,
The Book NOW Closed
Awaiting a NEW STORY to Unfold

DON'T GIVE UP

The Value of Life is so Precious
Sometimes we are Misguided by the True Essence
So many Amazing Qualities if you look within
Such great Opportunities for you to Win

I don't know your Story,
But I hope I can Shed some Insight
Be careful with whom you Engage,
Let no one Dim your Light

Sometimes when we Look in the Mirror
The Imperfections are so clear
Wondering why you were Created
To even be here

There may be Chastisement;
Relatable
But often times we miss what is
Truly Situational

I'm not sure if you are Spiritual
But what I can say
There's Comfort in knowing
Someone provides comfort Day after Day

Life isn't a Smooth Sailing event
Sometimes we get into things,
Obstacles that were meant

It's not a Road not Traveled
That you have to Avoid
It's the ones most Frequently Visited
While carrying a Load

It's the Road that once Displayed
Rainbows after the Rain
But now it's Encompassed
With so much Hurt and Pain

Let me Share some things with you
Some things that will Hopefully help Guide you
Remember this too Shall Pass
Years from now you May Not Remember; at last

You will see those Rainbows
Once Again
You will Dance in the Rain;
Don't Pretend

Smiles will again Resurface
Because your Cloudy Skies will display pictures,
Worth it

Flowers will Bloom, Seasons will Change
You will once again be able to Smell the Rain;
Quite Strange

Right now the Vision doesn't seem so Clear
Right now you see things differently
But as they Reappear

The Color will be Brighter,
NEVER Dull
The Clouds will be Scattered; Yes see the World

The screeching tires will once again,
Gain your Attention
The Reflection in the Mirror will be an Added Bonus
Did I mention

The girl smiling back
Will be Full of Grace
But it's not just any girl,
It's the one who Won this Race

PARENTING TIMES TWO

As a parent let me start by Declaring
What I'm bringing forth is Reality
Because of someone Caring

About Who you are and your Presentation
Don't take for Granted when you receive Love
In the form of a Different Relation

The topic here relates Divorce
And Encompasses Pain
But with Love in your Heart
We will give the Pain a New Name

Let me start at the Beginning for you
So that I can Align you with
What's True

Divorce states the following:
Coming to an End, to Separate

But it was Based upon a Union
In which God once helped Orchestrate
Let me see if I can Help you with Words
The reality of two who join together on One Accord

A Mommy and Daddy's Love
Is beyond compare
The first moment your Face met there's,
They couldn't help Admire and Stare

Something so Precious as a baby girl
Brought into their Lives
to add more Love to this World

The Beginning was a Start
That only they could Dream
But the Ending wasn't Planned and as it seems

You are Affected by the Ending
Which probably Hurts them More,
No need in Pretending

As parents we don't often Do Everything Right
Regardless of what one may see
There's a few things we keep
Hidden Out of Sight

What I'm saying is. . .
Even though this Process has been Hard
There's more to Include with added Regard

Your Feelings should always be Heard
Because what you have to say is Important,
I once Overheard

Divorce can make a child Withdraw
Or Change
It can Hurt, the pain feeling a Bit Strange

But that's only the Beginning, You see
If that parent moves on
Then the two become three, added Company

Baby girl what I can't Stress enough
Sometimes we think with our Head
And we hope our Heart can be Tough

We use Examples from others
And hope it Relates
But we don't ever want to Hurt our kids,
But we also want Love at any rate

If I can't leave you with anything else
Let me Utter this
Don't run away from Opportunity,
Embrace and Don't Miss

The chance to Increase your Love for each parent,
Remember, Stay True
Don't get Misguided,
Be Honest and let NOTHING Separate you
LOVE THEM BOTH!!

DID I?

Over the past several years
We've Built something Quite Special
A Connection Fulfilled
That's the Opposite of Artificial

It's hard to Move Past
Or let things Subside
Our Foundation is so Sturdy
And our Love, Trust, and Fulfillment is Applied

When you Truly Love someone
You don't want to see them Hurt
You Devote Time, Understanding, and Patience
Engulfed with each other's Support

Comfortable; Pleasant, Agreeable, Warm, Snug
From our Causal Text Messages
To our body to body naked Hugs

Your smile Warms my Heart,
Our exchanged Kisses touch my Soul
You are my Best Friend,
Whom I want to Love until Forever; I am told

When you really Love there's no Magic Wand
To make things Perfect
You adjust the Imperfections
Because they are Worth it

Never allow your Insecurities
To block your Blessing
Because there's No Fun when all through Life
There's Lots of Guessing

Did I not love as hard as I could?
Did I make sure there was no confusion,
And everything stated was understood?

Did I follow my Heart
Which was guided by Honesty?
Or did my Misjudgments Hinder me
From Progressing; Tragedy

As your Best Friend I never wanted to allow you
To get away
It's not so easy to feel Disconnected
Each and Every Day

The misfortune of going through life
Wondering and feeling Incomplete
But one must Understand in this Race called Life,
God didn't Intend for one to Experience Love
Where you have to Compete. . .

A WOMAN EMPOWERED

An Empowered Woman is Compelling. . .
And beautiful beyond Depiction
Encompassed with an Enchanted Charisma;
Overshadowing mere Description

She's Elegant, Prestigious, Captivating
A Woman of God so Intriguing, so Fascinating
Her presence is Divine, Structure created like no other
She Encompasses so many Layers. . .
The Depth is yet to be Detected

Full circle,
She has the Power to Create, Nurture, and Transform. . .
Its Preselected

Her thoughts Routed
In different Directions
Dreams painted on Canvas
With added Acquisitions

Her Appearance and Demeanor
Tells a unique Narrative
Adapting to Time, Place, and Occurrence;
That's Imperative

Let's journey through the Bible
And discuss women with relatable Circumstance

Mary of Nazareth; Modeled Obedience and Trust
Ruth a Widow; Faith and Bravery
Eve; accepting personal Responsibility
Rachel; Wronged, difficulty Conceiving
Hagar; Prejudice, Injustice, Despair
But through all the Pain and Suffering
God showed up to Repair

Proverbs 31:30:
Charm is Deceptive and Beauty is Fleeting;
But a woman who Fears the LORD is to be Praised
Purposefully Driven a woman of Virtue

You were Created
To Stand Out
Your Presence often Felt
Without Doubt

Your Ambition so Demanding
NOTHING Compared
Your Tenacity, Heroism, Confidence,
No Positive Characteristic Spared

You should now Understand how Generous
Your Heart can be
And how Spectacular your Existence
For all to See

Continue setting Standards and building Empires
The softness in your Eyes
In which others Admire

Take each day to Glam

Glorify

Lead

Awe

Make Anew

There's so many Great Things,

God has in store for you

Are you an Empowered Woman?

SALUTING YOUR SERVICE

November 11th
Honors those men and women
With unselfish acts
Bravery, Dedication, Fearlessness,
The depth of their Scars unmatched

Saluting:
Honor, Celebrate, Recognize, Admiration,
And Respect
Service:
The action of Helping, doing Work, Performing;
In Retrospect

Veteran:
Army, Navy, Air Force, Discharge, Noble
Basic Training, Agony, Sweat, Tears, Family
Disconnection; Body Immobile

Through research, I've Learned
the Language has Deciphered a bit
From attention to atten-hut;
Depending on the Cadence; befit

One may understand through
Humility and Sacrifice
A Veteran is Created

Molded, Embedded, Traditions Supported;
Respect Elevated

I'm reminded of a Bible verse,
Joshua reported this. . .

Have I commanded you?
Be strong and courageous, do not be afraid,
For the Lord your God will be with you
Wherever you go. . .

As we Salute you this day Veteran,
One won't take for Granted

The countless hours spent;
Did I make the best choice;
Confusion Orchestrated

The Gourmet Cuisine traded in
For a packaged (MRE) meal ready to eat
The long hours of Practicing
To be Uniformed on Repeat

Veterans accepted the responsibility
To defend America and uphold Statue
Saluting your Service an Honor
That is Due

PURPOSE

Purpose, Cause, Motive, Creation
Some say your Purpose will wake you up
Because of God's Elevation

Oh this is an Amazing Word
Even to Write about
The Complexity breaks it down
And the Honoring gives reason without Doubt

Knowing your Life's Purpose,
Is the first step Guided
Discovering meaning is Honoring the Creator
Your gift He provided

If your Purpose is truly Sought After
And Acknowledged
Is that when Life truly begins
Because of His promise?

It is intended through Action
And resolved by Determination
There's a difference between
Purpose and Duration

Duration; a Period of Time, a Term
Purpose; use me God, the time. . .
Unknown

When you have a Purpose,
It's IMPOSSIBLE to just Exist
There's so much to be done
And because of this

First Peter 2:9:
"But you are a chosen people a royal priesthood,
A Holy nation. . ."
Your Purpose can be Fulfilled
Because you are His creation
PURPOSEFUL LIFE!!

EFFECTIVE

Effective:

Actual, Essential, Successful,

And having a Lasting Impact

There are a couple of ways to explain being Effective. . .

Such as Communication. . .

Let's start with that

To Communicate Effectively

One has to Articulate

Rambling without Direction,

Doesn't set the Tone you wanted to Create

Effective Communication is

Giving everyone and Equal Chance

To share their Insight, Ideas

And offer their Stance

Communicating Effectively
Actually helps build Conversation
It promotes Growth by Listening without Interruption,
Lack of Concentration

Being Effective can also relate to
An individual need
As an Effective person, seek first to Understand
Then be understood; Agreed?

It helps promote Proactively
What you are trying to Convey
It builds Trust around believing in you
And the Words you say

When your Presentation matches the drive
For a specific topic
Then your audience will be Captivated
By your Knowledge. . .
EFFECTIVENESS

BOND

Bond:

An Agreement, Securely to something else, Fasten, Secure
Within the partnership you're filled
With a Love so Pure

A mother-daughter Bond grows through Life
With Admiration
It's a Blessing beyond measure
One Encompassed with the greatest Relation

The qualities a mother Possesses are passed down
To her Princess
The Reflection in the Mirror,
A beautiful creation Nonetheless

Ladies there's No Magical Book
That ensures you are Doing Right
There's no secret agenda Hidden
From your Hindsight

There's no How to Guide
Which helps you through the Quest
There's no Return Policy,
The sender Entrusting you; Blessed

There's no Copy and Paste function
From one to the next
There's no added Button to Block and Move her From
Troubles more Complex

But there's very Remarkable Attributes
A mother owns
She's at all times knowing her daughters mannerisms
Even realizing her Angry tones

She's witnessed Growth and Maturity
Through each passing day
This Bond unbreakable,
But she wouldn't have it any other way

Keep God close as your daughter carries out
The mission
Her purpose driven by God's amazing Vision

Be a strong Support,
Trust me Mom, she's going to need you
As there will be times where her Strength is Weak,
Her Heart is Broken and Tears block her View

Be a Listening ear, Wait your Turn
We often Teach but don't Practice
That's where Bonds Grow the Strongest
And the Fact is

Daughters help mom's Grow and even Mature
Since the Creation, you aren't the same you; you're
Stronger than Before

Wiser, Smarter even
Making better Choices, being a Strong Foundation
She can Believe in

DISAPPOINTMENT

Disappointment:
Defeat, Miscalculation, Bust, Setback
Feelings of Despair, Numbness,
Your Happiness a Struggle to Playback

I'm reminded of a few steps
That could help in Addition
As they begin with Favor from God
Included in the Decision

Step One:
Believe in God's plan as it was Created
Step Two:
Grieve when necessary your Feelings
Increasingly Validated
Step Three:
Pray and while doing so Seek and ye shall Find
Step Four:
Listen and Wait, the answer given is Always on Time

Step Five:

Search for the Good even during this Season

Lastly, Step Six:

Believe in Yourself because within your Purpose
There's Reason

Yes,
Even with those Six Steps Adversities will Arise. . .
But now you are more Equipped,
Your Thoughts and Focus; Emphasized!!!

She enters the room, every step Calculated
Inhaling/Exhaling slow shallows Breaths,
Sweat gleaming upon her; Orchestrated

She struggles to Speak, vastly consumed by Regrets
Clinched in each Swallow
Will she be able to Withstand her Nervousness,
Living each day Awaiting another Tomorrow

The time is now,
She's learning to Step Out in the Moment
Standing taller on the Stage, Fear diminishing,
She's owning it

The topic brought forth is Self-love,
Which is Essential
Please listen to these Main Characteristics;
It's Influential

Self-love is the mere Foundation of the Level
In which you'll love someone else
It's dynamic, it grows in ways
That mature One's self

In order to appreciate what Self-love
Can decree
You have to have the Secret Ingredients
To Love inwardly

Step 1:

Live intentionally; NO DAY is Promised,

But the Promise of the Purpose

Makes things Honest

Step 2:

Forgive often, it helps alleviate Stress. . .

You can produce Lines and Wrinkles

Don't do that to yourself

Step 3:

Act on needs Versus wants,

He or she may Speak to your Mind,

But what about your Heart

Step 4:

Protect yourself, listen to your emotions.. your heart

won't mislead

Step 5:

Be aware;

Understand that certain things bother you. . .

Then Proceed

The increase of Self-love has to
Begin right now
Every Flaw, every Imperfection,
Created you somehow

From every Strand of Hair,
Every Wrinkle just Right
To every Dimple that's in Plain View,
And the ones Out of Sight

Take time to Count Joys; Breathless
Enjoy your favorite hobbies; Be Relentless

Change can be Good; Transparency
Devote your Time, but do so Sparingly

She exists, Pure Admiration,
Because this is her Inheritance
Self-love. . .No Negativity, just Excellence

A WALK TO REMEMBER

Faith the size of a Mustard Seed
Believing that's all the Reliance
In which she needs

A woman who heard about a man
Who performed Countless Miracles
Across the Land

Her journey began with a walk. . .

Here's her Story
Bearing fruit; Productivity
The woman selected Worthy,
Yet regarded without Sensitivity

Who is this woman of Faith desperate of being Healed
Following Countless Interactions with physicians,
Money spent, Sickness worsened,
Body without Shield

Twelve years of Suffering,
Agony and Uncertainty,
Paints a picture of a woman
With an issue of Blood Worthily

She is unnamed but her story is Evolutionary
A woman deemed Unclean
But with Modesty and Humility
She became Legendary

Her infirmity was her Identity,
Existence
A disease Longstanding;
Persistence

The thought of being Cured with a Simple Touch
Is Unthinkable
The Tenacity in her eyes I imagine,
Indescribable

If only I could Touch the Hem
As her options of being Healed
Were growing Dim

That Glimpse of Faith
Was unlike anything Familiar
But once dried up,
The cleanliness Convicted her

Oh His WILL made Perfect
Once a battered woman,
So Undeserving. . .
Now she feels Worth it

Strength, Power, and Faith
Allowed her to Persevere
Praying one day soon her Pain
Would Disappear

This anonymous woman chained by Sickness
Yet through Trials and Tribulations
She remained Relentless

Through Adversities in which she had
To Overcome
A Miracle happened
Now her battle has been Won
A WALK TO REMEMBER!!!

ABOUT THE AUTHOR

With tears in my eyes I write this, I absolutely love writing, it's my safe haven. I'm from a small town, somewhere between the site of the Branch Davidians and Baylor University I sit, a mother, a daughter, a sister, a friend, a writer. I enjoy worshipping God, family time, traveling, reading, and spending as much time as possible with my heart in human form.

In these stories you will find all walks of life, some of my own, some of others, but most importantly I hope you feel each one and relate to the message.

Thank you for taking the time to read, may God bless you richly!

CPSIA information can be obtained
at www.ICGtesting.com
Printed in the USA
LVHW050555200820
663704LV00014B/409

9 781734 901450